FOOLPROOF INDIAN COOKERY

MADHUR JAFFREY

FOOLPROOF INDIAN COOKERY

MADHUR JAFFREY

Step by step to

everyone's favourite

Indian recipes

Food photography by Jean Cazals

Published by BBC Worldwide Ltd,
Woodlands, 80 Wood Lane,
London W12 0TT

First published 2001
Copyright © Madhur Jaffrey 2001
The moral right of the author has been asserted.

Food photography © Jean Cazals 2001

ISBN 0 563 53737 X

Commissioning editor: Nicky Copeland
Project editor: Sarah Lavelle
Copy editor: Jane Middleton
Art direction: Lisa Pettibone and Sarah Ponder
Designer: Sarah Jackson
Home economist: Marie Ange Lapierre
Stylist: Sue Rowlands

Set in Univers
Printed and bound in Italy by L.E.G.O spa
Colour separations by Kestrel Digital Colour, Chelmsford

Contents

Introduction

When I left India to study at the Royal Academy of Dramatic Art in London, I could not cook at all. Magnificent meals had always appeared miraculously at our table under my mother's watchful, supervisory eye. Even though she was a formidable cook herself, once she had married into my father's family she was encouraged to leave daily cooking to others. On religious festival days she could hardly contain herself and would go quietly into the kitchen and start making all the speciality sweets and savouries herself. I watched her with great awe but never participated.

If I had not left home I probably would never have learned to cook. In London I yearned for home cooking and wrote pleading letters to my mother to teach me the fundamentals. This she did in regular airmail letters, which I still have. This correspondence course lasted several years. My mother had to teach me how to make rice, tea, the lot. I had far to go.

I mention my own humble and faltering beginnings in this field because I want to encourage you to cook Indian food. If my mother could teach me, a complete ignoramus, the least I can do is pass on her valuable lessons to you.

Ingredients and Equipment

INGREDIENTS

Common Indian ingredients, which once required visits to far-flung groceries, are now available in most Western supermarkets. What is even better, many websites offer them by mail order as well. Here is a guide to the ingredients I have used in this book.

Bay leaves
Dried bay leaves are added to scores of Indian rice and meat dishes for their delicate aroma. Sometimes they are lightly browned in oil first to intensify this aroma.

Left to right: *masoor dal* (red split lentils) and *mung dal* (yellow split peas)

Beans and peas, dried
All dried beans and peas should be stored in tightly closed jars, then picked over and washed in several changes of water before use.

Masoor dal (red split lentils)
A hulled, salmon-coloured pea that turns yellow after cooking.

Mung (or *moong*) *dal*
These yellow split peas are sold both with and without their skins by almost every Indian grocer. The skins are green, the flesh yellow. Only the hulled and split peas are required in this book.

Black pepper
Native to India, whole peppercorns are added to rice and meat dishes to give a mild peppery-lemony flavour. Ground pepper was once used in large amounts, sometimes several tablespoons in a single dish, especially in southern India where it grows. The arrival of the chilli pepper from the New World in around 1498 supplanted it to some extent, though black pepper is still a popular spice. In some southern Indian dishes, peppercorns are lightly roasted before use to draw out their lemony taste.

Cardamom
Small green cardamom pods, the fruit of a plant similar to ginger, contain clusters of black, highly aromatic seeds that smell like a combination of camphor, eucalyptus, orange peel and lemon. Whole pods are added to rice and meat dishes, while ground seeds are one of the main flavours in *garam masala*. Green cardamom pods are the most aromatic. White ones, sold by supermarkets, have been bleached and have less flavour.

This versatile spice is the vanilla of India, and is used in most desserts and sweetmeats.

Clockwise from top: cumin seeds, cinnamon stick, whole and ground nutmeg, mace, cardamom pods, cloves, black peppercorns

Clockwise from top left: cardamom pods, ground cardamom seed, whole cardamom seed

It is also added to spiced tea and sucked as a mouth freshener. Cardamom seeds that have been removed from their pods are sold separately by Indian grocers. If you cannot get them, take the seeds out of the pods yourself. If ground cardamom is called for, you can grind a tablespoon of the seeds in a spice grinder or a clean coffee grinder, or you can buy it ready ground.

Cashew nuts
These nuts travelled from the Americas via Africa and India all the way to China. They are grown commonly on India's west coast and are used in pilafs, desserts and even made into *bhajias* and curries.

Cayenne pepper
This fiery powder is made today by grinding the dried red skins of several types of chilli peppers. In India, and in Indian grocers in the West, it is simply called chilli powder.

But since that name can be confused with the Mexican-style chilli powder, which also contains cumin, garlic and oregano, I have used the name 'cayenne pepper' in all the recipes in this book. Use your discretion when adding it to your cooking, as it is very hot.

Chapati flour
Sold by all Indian grocers, this is a very finely ground wheatmeal flour used to make *chapatis*, *pooris* and other breads.

Chickpea flour
A very fine and nutritionally rich flour made out of ground chickpeas. It is sold by Indian grocers and some large supermarkets and wholefood stores, and is sometimes labelled gram flour or *besan*.

Chillies, dried
When whole dried chillies are added to Indian food, it is generally done through the *tarka* method, in which the hot chillies are first dropped into very hot oil (see Tarka dal on page 86). Quick contact with the oil enhances and intensifies the flavour of their skins. It is that flavour that Indians want (Mexicans traditionally bring out the flavour by roasting their dried chillies before use). Then, if actual chilli heat is desired, the chillies are allowed to stew with the food being cooked.

The most common dried chilli in India is a hot, red cayenne type. There is a variety of red chilli, known as the Kashmiri chilli, used for the bright red colour it imparts, rather like good paprika. Since it is not always easy to obtain in the West, I often use a combination of cayenne pepper and paprika in my recipes.

Chillies, fresh
The fresh green chilli most commonly used in Indian cooking is a cayenne type, generally about 7.5 cm (3 in) long and slender. Its heat can vary from mild to fiery – careless bees, it seems, unthinkingly cross-pollinate different varieties that grow close together. The only way to judge the heat of a chilli is by tasting a tiny piece of skin from the middle section (keep some yoghurt handy!). The top part of the chilli, which contains more seeds, is always the hottest, the bottom tip the

Above: fresh red and green chillies, cayenne pepper

mildest. The hot seeds are never removed in India but you may do so if you prefer.

Use whatever type of chilli you can find. The jalapeño is thicker skinned and often hotter than the Indian chilli. Use discretion, and be sure to wash your hands well after handling chillies. If you touch your eyes, mouth or nose without washing, they may burn.

Fresh red chillies are just green chillies that have ripened. However, their flavour is slightly different, though their intensity can be exactly the same. All chillies are a very rich source of iron and vitamins A and C.

To store fresh chillies, wrap them first in newspaper, then in plastic, and keep them in the refrigerator. They should keep for several weeks. Any that begin to soften and rot should be removed, as they tend to infect the whole batch.

Cinnamon

Used mainly for desserts in the West, cinnamon, often in its 'stick' form, is added to many Indian rice and meat dishes for its warm, sweet aroma. This inner bark from a laurel-like tree is also an important ingredient in the aromatic spice mixture, *garam masala*.

Cloves

Indians rarely use cloves in desserts but do use them in meat and rice dishes and in the spice mixture, *garam masala*. They carry pungently aromatic cloves as well as cardamom pods in tiny silver boxes, to use as mouth-fresheners when needed. For the same reason, cloves are always part of the betel leaf paraphernalia that is offered as a digestive at the end of a meal.

Coconut milk

I have used only canned coconut milk in the recipes in this book. It is available at most Asian groceries but the quality varies. Once you have found a brand you like, stick to it. There is one called Chaokah, from Thailand, which I like very much and use frequently. It is white, creamy and quite delicious.

As the cream tends to rise to the top in the can, always stir coconut milk well before use. Sometimes, because of the fat in it, canned coconut milk can become very grainy. You

can either whizz it for a second in a blender or beat it well. Canned coconut milk does not keep well once it has been opened. Its refrigerated life is no longer than two days.

Coriander, fresh

This is the parsley of India. It is ground into fresh chutneys, mixed with vegetables, cooked with chicken and used as a garnish.

Generally, only the delicate, fragrant green leaves are used, though southern Indians often throw the stalks into soupy *dals* for extra flavour. It should be very well washed first. When fresh coriander is called for, chop up the top of the plant where the stalks are slender. You will have to pick off the leaves from the lower half, where the stalks are thicker. The best way to keep fresh coriander is to stand it in a glass of water, cover it with a plastic bag and refrigerate the whole thing. Break off the leaves and stems you need and keep the rest refrigerated. The water should be changed daily and dead leaves removed.

Coriander seeds

These beige, ridged seeds are sweetly spicy and cheap to buy. As a result they are used in a great deal of Indian cookery, and constitute the major part of many spice mixtures. In Maharashtra (western India), they are combined with cumin, shredded coconut and other spices, then dry-roasted and ground to make a delicious 'black *masala*' that is used with both meat and vegetables. In the southern state of Kerala, they are combined with fenugreek seeds, black peppercorns and red chillies, dry-roasted and used to flavour prawn and lobster dishes. In the north, coriander, cumin and turmeric are a common trinity added to hundreds of dishes.

To dry-roast coriander seeds, put them into a small, hot cast-iron frying pan. Stir over a medium heat for 2–3 minutes, until they turn a few shades darker and give off a roasted aroma. To grind the seeds, it is best to use a spice grinder or clean coffee grinder.

Cumin seeds

These look like caraway seeds but are slightly larger, plumper and lighter in colour. Their flavour is similar to caraway, only gentler and sweeter, and they are used both whole and ground. When whole, they are often subjected

Above, from top: cinnamon sticks, coriander seeds, cloves

Clockwise from top: fennel seeds, cumin seeds, fenugreek seeds, brown mustard seeds

to the *tarka* technique, which requires dropping them into very hot oil for a few seconds (see Tarka dal on page 86). This intensifies their flavour and makes them slightly nutty. When ground, they are used in meat, rice and vegetable dishes.

Cumin seeds can also be dry-roasted before grinding, in the same way as coriander seeds (see page 12). This version is sprinkled over many snack foods, relishes and yoghurt dishes.

Black cumin seeds are a rare and therefore more expensive form of cumin. They are sweeter, smaller and more delicate, and their mild pungency is perfect for the aromatic mixture of spices known as *garam masala*. The seeds can also be lightly dry-roasted and sprinkled whole over rice pilafs.

Curry powder

This is a spice mixture using sometimes more than 20 spices. It has never been standardized, so there are hundreds of variations. Of all the commercial ones, my favourite is Bolst, which comes in mild, medium and hot varieties.

Fennel seeds

These look a bit like cumin seeds but are much plumper and greener. Their flavour is decidedly anise-like. In Kashmir they are often ground and used in conjunction with asafoetida and ground ginger for a host of fish and vegetable dishes. In northern and western India, the whole seeds are added to pickles and chutneys and snack foods. They are also used in vegetable stir-fries, particularly in Bengal (eastern India), where they are part of the five-spice mixture called *panchphoran*. Fennel seeds can also be dry-roasted (see Coriander seeds, page 12) and then eaten after a meal as both a digestive and a mouth freshener.

Fenugreek seeds

It is these angular, yellowish seeds that give many commercial curry powders their earthy, musky 'curry' aroma. In most of northern India they are used mainly in pickles, chutneys and vegetarian dishes. In western, southern and eastern India they are added to meat and fish dishes as well (such as the *vindaloo* from Goa). They are part of the Bengali spice mixture, *panchphoran*.

Garam masala

This spice combination varies with each household, though the name seems constant. *Garam* means 'hot' and *masala* means 'spices', so the spices in this mixture were traditionally those that 'heated' the body according to the ancient Ayurvedic system of medicine. They all happen to be highly aromatic as well. Commercial mixtures tend to cut down on the expensive cardamom and fill up with the cheaper coriander and cumin. Here is how you make a classic ground mixture:

In a clean spice grinder or coffee grinder, combine 1 tablespoon cardamom seeds, 1 teaspoon cloves, 1 teaspoon black peppercorns, 1 teaspoon black cumin seeds, a 5 cm (2 in) piece of cinnamon stick, ⅛ nutmeg and a curl of mace. Grind the spices until you have a fine powder. Store in a tightly closed jar and use as needed. Many people add a bay leaf to the mixture. Generally, though not always, *garam masala* is sprinkled on a dish towards the end of the cooking time to retain its aroma.

The *garam masala* spices can also be used whole. If two or more of them are used together, they are still loosely referred to as *garam masala*.

It is not essential to make your own *garam masala*, unless you prefer to. Indian grocers sell a fairly decent version.

Garlic

Some Indians (Kashmiri Hindus and the Jain sect) do not touch garlic, but the rest of the country eats it with pleasure. It is an important ingredient in meat sauces, which often require onion, garlic and ginger, the 'wet' trinity of seasonings, to be ground to a paste and then fried in oil until dark and thick. In parts of Saurashtra (western India), garlic, salt and dried red chillies are pounded together to make an everyday condiment.

Ghee (clarified butter)

This is butter that has been so thoroughly clarified that it can even be used for deep-frying without burning. As it no longer contains milk solids, refrigeration is not necessary. It has a nutty, buttery taste. All Indian grocers sell *ghee* and I find it more convenient to buy it. If, however, you need

Above: garlic and fresh coriander

to make it, melt 450 g (1 lb) unsalted butter in a pan over a low heat and let it simmer very gently until the milky solids turn brownish and cling to the sides of the pan or else fall to the bottom. The time that this takes will depend on the amount of water in the butter. Watch carefully towards the end and do not let it burn. Strain the *ghee* through a triple layer of muslin. Home-made *ghee* is best stored in the refrigerator.

Ginger

This rhizome has a sharp, pungent, cleansing taste and is a digestive to boot. It can be ground to a paste and used in meat sauces (see Garlic, page 15) and in drinks. It is also cut into slivers or minute dice and added to the pan when stir-frying potatoes, green beans, spinach and other vegetables.

When finely grated ginger is required, it should first be peeled and then grated on the finest part of the grater so it turns into pulp. If a recipe specifies 2.5 cm (1 in) fresh root ginger for grating, it is best to keep that piece attached to the large knob. The knob acts as a handle and saves you from grating your fingers.

Ginger should be stored in a cool, dry place. Many people like to bury it in dryish, sandy soil. This way they can break off and retrieve small portions as they need them, while the rest of the knob generously keeps growing.

Mustard seeds, brown

Of the three varieties of mustard seeds – white (actually yellowish), brown (a reddish-brown) and black (slightly larger, brownish-black seeds) – it is the brown that has been grown and used in India since antiquity. To confuse matters, the brown seeds are often referred to as black. When shopping, look for the small, reddish-brown variety, although at a pinch any sort will do.

All mustard seeds have Jekyll and Hyde characteristics. When crushed, they are nose-tinglingly pungent. However, if they are thrown into hot oil and allowed to pop, they turn quite nutty and sweet. In India both these techniques are used, sometimes in the same recipe. Whole mustard seeds, popped in oil, are used to season vegetables, pulses, yoghurt relishes, salads and rice dishes. Crushed seeds are added to sauces, pickles and when steaming fish.

Nutmeg and mace

Nutmeg is the dried seed of a round, pear-like fruit. Mace is the red, lacy covering around the seed that turns yellowish when dried. Both have a similar warm, sweetish and slightly camphoric flavour, though mace has a faintly bitter edge.

Both nutmeg and mace are used in the *garam masala* mixture on page 15. A nutmeg breaks quite easily. Just hit it lightly with a hammer to get the third needed for the *garam masala*. Indians almost never use nutmeg for desserts and drinks.

Oil

Although it is not traditional, I like to use a pale, light olive oil (not extra virgin) in the recipes in this book, as it is low in saturates and neutral in flavour. Groundnut and

Above: fresh ginger, okra, turmeric

Above: raw squid and fresh, raw prawns

safflower oil are also suitable. If oil is used for deep-frying, it can be re-used. Skim off all extraneous matter with a skimmer and then drop a chunk of ginger or potato into the oil and let it fry. This chunk will absorb a lot of the unwanted flavours. When it is cool enough, strain the oil through a triple thickness of muslin or a large handkerchief. Let it cool completely and then store it in a bottle. When re-using, mix the old oil half and half with fresh oil.

Okra

Choose young, tender okra pods with small seeds. Wipe them with a damp cloth and spread them out to dry off before cutting them. To trim the pods, discard the very top and the tip.

Paprika

Although it is not a common part of the Indian kitchen, I use paprika frequently to give dishes their traditional red colour. Since it is only for colour, it is important to buy good-quality paprika that is bright red. Paprika tends to darken as it sits in glass bottles, so buy it in a tin or store it in a cupboard.

Poppadums

Also called *papar*, these crispy wafers are served with most Indian meals but are also good with drinks. They are generally made out of dried split peas, and are sold either plain or studded with black pepper (or garlic or red pepper) by Indian grocers. They should be deep-fried for a few seconds in hot oil (see page 32) or toasted.

Prawns

Only raw prawns should be used for the dishes in this book. The kind that I prefer are sold without heads but still in their shells. You can also buy them peeled, if you so wish. I generally find that medium-sized prawns are the sweetest.

To peel and de-vein prawns, first pull off the legs, then peel off the shell. The tail end usually needs to be pulled off. With a sharp knife, make a shallow slit along the length of the prawn where its backbone might have been and pull out the dark thread.

It is a good idea to wash prawns with salt before cooking. This removes any sliminess and refreshes them. Put the peeled prawns in a bowl, sprinkle a tablespoon or so of coarse or kosher salt over them and rub them lightly. Then wash them in cold water. Repeat one more time, rinsing well to ensure that all the salt is washed away. Drain the prawns and lightly pat dry with kitchen paper. Store in a covered bowl or polythene bag in the refrigerator until needed.

Rice

Many varieties of rice are used in Indian cookery. There is the protein-rich, partially milled 'red' rice popular along the Konkan coast, south of Bombay. Then there is 'boiled' rice. This is the original parboiled rice that predates Uncle Ben and must have been the inspiration for the rice Uncle Ben produced in 1943. Along India's southern coasts, 'boiled' rice has been produced for over a century. The process of boiling the rice before it is husked and milled not only makes the grains tough and indestructible but also pushes the B-complex vitamins into the inner kernel. This rice is used not only for everyday eating in the south but also to make a variety of pancakes, cakes and snacks.

Then there is basmati rice, the pearls of the north. It is a highly aromatic, very fine long-grain rice grown in the foothills of the Himalayan mountains. The better varieties are generally aged for a year before being sold. For cooking perfect basmati rice, see page 98.

Shallots

These are used routinely in southern India in place of the larger onion common to the north. In places like Goa, they hang in kitchens like long ropes, to be plucked at will.

Squid

I like to buy small, tender squid with bodies no larger than 15 cm (6 in). Many oriental grocers sell cleaned, frozen squid. Just thaw them out, cut them as required and they are ready to be used. If you buy them from a fishmonger and they have not been cleaned, you need to do the task yourself. It is quite easy.

To clean squid, twist off the head (with the tentacles). The inner body sac will probably come away with it. If it does not, pull it out.

Discard the sac and the hard eye area, which you may have to cut off with a knife. Retain the tentacles. If possible, pull off some of the brownish skin on the tentacles. (You may safely leave this, if you wish.) Peel the brownish skin from the tube-like body. Discard this skin and pull out the smooth inner cartilage (or pen). The squid can now be washed and used as your recipe requires. It can either be cut into rings or opened up and cut into strips.

Turmeric

A rhizome, like ginger, only with smaller, more delicate 'fingers', fresh turmeric is quite orange inside. When dried, it turns bright yellow. It is this musky powder that gives some Indian dishes a yellowish cast. As it is cheap and is also considered to be an antiseptic, it is used freely in the cooking of pulses, vegetables and meats. Both the fresh and the dried form are used in India. In the West, we generally get the dried powder. If you have access to Indian grocer's shops, try using fresh turmeric. A 2.5 cm (1 in) piece is equal to about ½ teaspoon of ground turmeric. Just like ginger, it needs to be peeled and ground. This grinding is best done with the help of a little water in an electric blender.

EQUIPMENT

While Indian food does not really require any special utensils or gadgets, it does help to have the following:

Karhai or wok

A *karhai* is the Indian equivalent of the Chinese wok. They are both all-purpose utensils that may be used for stir-frying, steaming, simmering or deep-frying. A *karhai* or wok is traditionally a round-bottomed pan, with the *karhai* being more like a half moon and a wok being more open. A round-bottomed *karhai* or wok works well on a gas hob. Because of its shape, flames can encircle it and allow it to heat quickly and efficiently. If you are cooking on an electric hob, you may prefer a wok with a flatter bottom. A *karhai* or wok is very economical for deep-frying, as it will hold a good depth of oil without needing the quantity a straight-sided pan would require. It is also ideal for stir-frying, as foods can be vigorously tossed around in it. As they hit nothing but well-heated surfaces, they cook fast and retain their moisture at the same time.

What kind of *karhai* or wok should you buy? Traditional Indian *karhais* are generally made out of cast iron but non-stick ones are now available as well. They come in all sizes, and what you buy depends upon the kind of cooking you do. Traditional Chinese woks of good quality are made either of thin tempered iron or carbon steel. The ideal wok is 35 cm (14 in) in diameter and fairly deep (shallow, saucer-shaped woks are quite useless).

Seasoning a *karhai* or wok

The iron and carbon-steel versions leave the factory coated with oil. This needs to be scrubbed off with a cream or powder cleanser. Then they need to be seasoned. Rinse well in water and set over a low heat. Now brush all over with about 2 tablespoons of vegetable oil and leave over a low heat for 10–15 minutes. Wipe off the oil with a piece of kitchen paper. Brush with more oil and repeat the process 3 or 4 times. The *karhai* or wok is now seasoned. Do not scrub it again after use; just wash with hot water and then wipe dry. It will *not* have a scrubbed look. It will, however, become more and more 'non-stick' as it is used.

Cast-iron frying pans

I find a 13 cm (5 in) cast-iron frying pan ideal for roasting spices and a large one perfect for pan-grilling thin slices of meat. All cast-iron frying pans can be heated without any liquid and they retain an even temperature. They need to be seasoned in exactly the same way as a *karhai* or wok (see opposite). Once properly seasoned, they should never be scrubbed with abrasive cleaners.

Tava

A *tava* is a slightly curved cast-iron griddle, used for making Indian breads, such as the *parathas* on page 108.

Blender, spice grinder, mortar and pestle

In India, pestles and grinding stones of varying shapes, sizes and materials are used to pulverize everything from cumin seeds to hot dried red chillies. I find it much easier to use a powerful electric blender for wet ingredients and a clean electric spice grinder or coffee grinder for dry ones. For small quantities, you might still want to use a heavy mortar and pestle.

Left to right: electric deep-fat fryer, coffee grinder, rice cooker

Above: *karhai*, cast-iron frying pan, pestle and mortar, nutmeg grater, wooden ginger grater

Grater

The Japanese make a special grater for ginger (and Japanese horseradish) which produces a fine pulp. It has tiny, hair-like spikes that are perfect for this purpose. If you ever come across one, do buy it. Otherwise, use the finest part of an ordinary grater for grating fresh ginger.

Electric rice cooker

If you regularly cook large amounts of rice, an electric rice cooker can be a useful investment. Its main use is to free all burners on the hob for other purposes and make the cooking of rice an easy, almost mindless task. I have one, which I use only for plain rice.

Electric deep-fat fryer

For those who are nervous of deep-frying, an electric fryer is a godsend. Because it is thermostatically controlled, and has a lid that closes over the splattering food, this piece of equipment helps to make deep-frying a painless, safe and clean task.

Conversion tables

Conversions are approximate and have been rounded up or down. Follow one set of measurements only – do not mix metric and Imperial.

Weights		Volume		Measurements	
Metric	**Imperial**	**Metric**	**Imperial**	**Metric**	**Imperial**
15 g	½ oz	25 ml	1 fl oz	0.5 cm	¼ inch
25 g	1 oz	50 ml	2 fl oz	1 cm	½ inch
40 g	1½ oz	85 ml	3 fl oz	2.5 cm	1 inch
50 g	2 oz	150 ml	5 fl oz (¼ pint)	5 cm	2 inches
75 g	3 oz	300 ml	10 fl oz (½ pint)	7.5 cm	3 inches
100 g	4 oz	450 ml	15 fl oz (¾ pint)	10 cm	4 inches
150 g	5 oz	600 ml	1 pint	15 cm	6 inches
175 g	6 oz	700 ml	1¼ pints	18 cm	7 inches
200 g	7 oz	900 ml	1½ pints	20 cm	8 inches
225 g	8 oz	1 litres	1¾ pints	23 cm	9 inches
250 g	9 oz	1.2 litres	2 pints	25 cm	10 inches
275 g	10 oz	1.25 litres	2¼ pints	30 cm	12 inches
350 g	12 oz	1.5 litres	2½ pints		
375 g	13 oz	1.6 litres	2¾ pints	**Oven temperatures**		
400 g	14 oz	1.75 litres	3 pints	140°C	275°F	Gas Mk 1
425 g	15 oz	1.8 litres	3¼ pints	150°C	300°F	Gas Mk 2
450 g	1 lb	2 litres	3½ pints	160°C	325°F	Gas Mk 3
550 g	1¼ lb	2.1 litres	3¾ pints	180°C	350°F	Gas Mk 4
675 g	1½ lb	2.25 litres	4 pints	190°C	375°F	Gas Mk 5
900 g	2 lb	2.75 litres	5 pints	200°C	400°F	Gas Mk 6
1.5 kg	3 lb	3.4 litres	6 pints	220°C	425°F	Gas Mk 7
1.75 kg	4 lb	3.9 litres	7 pints	230°C	450°F	Gas Mk 8
2.25 kg	5 lb	5 litres	8 pints (1 gal)	240°C	475°F	Gas Mk 9

SOUPS and STARTERS

Summery yoghurt soup

A perfect soup for a hot summer's day. You can have all the ingredients ready ahead of time and combine them at the last minute. To peel the tomatoes, take a sharp paring knife and peel each one in a circular pattern, just as you would an apple. To remove the seeds, cut the tomato crossways in half and gently squeeze out the seeds. If you wish to save time, you may omit this peeling and seeding and just go on to the dicing.

serves 4
preparation time: 15 minutes
cooking time: 20 minutes

4 new potatoes, unpeeled (use smallish ones)

1 tablespoon olive oil

½ teaspoon brown mustard seeds

600 ml (1 pint) plain yoghurt

900 ml (1½ pints) good-quality chicken stock, degreased and strained through a fine sieve

6 tablespoons single cream

8 tablespoons finely diced peeled cucumber

2 tomatoes, peeled, seeded and diced

⅛–¼ teaspoon cayenne pepper (depending how hot you like it)

2 teaspoons very finely chopped fresh dill

salt and freshly ground black pepper

1 Boil the new potatoes for 15–20 minutes, until tender, then drain and leave to cool. Peel and cut them into small dice.

2 Put the oil into a very small pan and set it over a medium-high heat. When it is very hot, put in the mustard seeds. As soon as they begin to pop, pour the oil and seeds into a large bowl.

3 Add the yoghurt to the bowl and beat it lightly with a whisk until smooth and creamy, then slowly whisk in the stock and cream. Then add all the remaining ingredients, including the potatoes, and mix them in with a wooden spoon. Chill until ready to serve.

Easy mulligatawny soup

A wonderful Anglo-Indian soup, this may be served as a first course or as a light lunch.

To grate ginger for this recipe, peel just a knob of the rhizome, hold the whole piece firmly and grate the peeled knob on the finest section of the grater. Garlic may be crushed in a garlic press.

Stir the soup well before serving as all *dal* soups tend to separate slightly.

serves 4–6
preparation time: 15 minutes
cooking time: 50 minutes

3 tablespoons olive or groundnut oil

1 teaspoon fresh root ginger, grated to a pulp

1 teaspoon garlic, crushed to a pulp

1 teaspoon ground cumin

1 teaspoon ground coriander

1½ teaspoons curry powder

⅛–¼ teaspoon cayenne pepper (depending how hot you like it)

200 g (7 oz) skinned and boned chicken thighs, cut into 1 cm (½ inch) dice

175 g (6 oz) red split lentils (*masoor dal*), picked over, washed and drained

1.2 litres (2 pints) chicken stock

1 teaspoon salt, or to taste

about 1 tablespoon fresh lemon juice

1 tablespoon finely chopped fresh coriander

1 Heat the oil in a heavy-based pan over a medium-high heat. When it is hot, put in the ginger and the garlic and stir for 10 seconds. Add the cumin, coriander, curry powder and cayenne and stir for another 10 seconds, then put in the diced chicken and stir for 30 seconds.

2 Add the split lentils, chicken stock and salt and bring to the boil. Partly cover the pan, reduce the heat to low and simmer for 45 minutes or until the lentils are very soft.

3 Add the lemon juice and fresh coriander and stir to mix in well.

Spinach and okra soup

The first time I had this soup was in the home of a Trinidad Indian. Instead of spinach, my host had used the large leaves of the taro root. This delicious creation may be served as either a first course at dinner or a main dish for lunch.

Okra is essential here as it binds the soup together, rather like a New Orleans gumbo. It should be washed and patted dry before cutting.

serves 4–6
preparation time: 20 minutes
cooking time: 45 minutes

4 tablespoons olive or groundnut oil

1 onion, coarsely chopped

3 garlic cloves, coarsely chopped

1 small carrot, cut into coarse rounds

10 green beans, cut into 2.5 cm (1 in) pieces

6 okra pods, trimmed at the ends and cut crossways into coarse slices

450 g (1 lb) fresh spinach, well washed and cut crossways into strips 1 cm (½ in wide)

1–2 hot green chillies, coarsely sliced

750 ml (1¼ pints) chicken stock

400 ml (14 fl oz) can of coconut milk, well stirred

salt and freshly ground black pepper

1 Put the oil in a large pan and set it over a medium-high heat. When it is hot, put in the onion, garlic, carrot, green beans and okra. Sauté for 5 minutes.

2 Now put in the spinach and chillies and cook for another 5 minutes. Pour in the stock, stir and bring to the boil. Cover the pan, reduce the heat to low and simmer gently for 25–30 minutes.

3 Put the soup in a food processor or blender and blend coarsely or finely, as desired. You will need to do this in several batches. Return the soup to the pan. Add the coconut milk and some salt and pepper to taste. Stir well and bring to a simmer before serving.

Fried poppadums

Poppadums have been part of Indian meals since ancient times, adding both a crunchy texture and nutritional value to the humblest of repasts. The ones you buy 'raw' are actually partly prepared. The manufacturers start with a split-pea dough, which they can leave plain or flavour with black pepper, chillies or garlic. They make small patties out of the dough and roll them out into thin discs, rather like *chapatis*. These discs are then dried in the sun. They still need to be roasted or fried. Here is the frying method.

Poppadums expand during frying, so make sure you allow plenty of room in the pan.

serves 6
preparation time: 1–2 minutes
cooking time: about 5 minutes

groundnut oil for deep-frying
6 poppadums

1 Pour some oil into a large frying pan to a depth of 2 cm (¾ in) and set it over a medium heat. When the oil is very hot, put in a poppadum (or half a poppadum, depending upon size). It will sizzle and expand in seconds.

2 Remove the poppadum with a slotted spoon and drain on kitchen paper. Cook the remaining poppadums in the same way.

Spicy cashews

There is nothing as good as freshly fried cashews. My mother always made them herself for my father, to accompany his evening drink during the winter months. After frying, she would let them drain briefly on thick brown paper, from the same batch she used to cover all our books, and then she served them in bowls made out of coconut shells. She just sprinkled salt and black pepper on them but I add a little cayenne pepper as well.

The frying oil may be reused.

serves 4–6
preparation time: 5 minutes
cooking time: 2–3 minutes

olive, vegetable or groundnut
  oil for deep-frying
225 g (8 oz) raw cashew nuts
¼ teaspoon salt
⅛ teaspoon cayenne pepper
freshly ground black pepper

1 Put a sieve on top of a metal bowl and set aside. Pour some oil into a deep frying pan to a depth of about 2.5 cm (1 in) and set it over a medium heat. When the oil is very hot, put in all the cashews. Fry them, stirring, until they turn a reddish-gold colour (this happens quite fast).

2 Empty the contents of the frying pan into the sieve to drain off the oil, then scatter the cashews over a baking tray lined with kitchen paper.

3 Sprinkle the salt, cayenne and some black pepper over the cashews while they are still hot and mix well. Serve warm or at room temperature.

Potato bhajias

Both the potatoes and their skins are used in these *bhajias*. Great for snacking and as a first course, they are generally served with a chutney, such as the Fresh green chutney on page 104 – or with tomato ketchup!

serves 4–6
preparation time: 10 minutes
cooking time: 15–20 minutes

For the batter:

100 g (4 oz) chickpea flour (also called gram flour or *besan*)

¼ teaspoon bicarbonate of soda

½ teaspoon ground turmeric

½ teaspoon cayenne pepper

½ teaspoon ground coriander

¾ teaspoon salt

1 teaspoon cumin seeds

about 250 ml (8 fl oz) water

2 potatoes, well scrubbed

groundnut oil for deep-frying

1 To make the batter, sift the chickpea flour, bicarbonate of soda, spices and salt into a large bowl. Add the cumin seeds, then gradually pour in the water, stirring as you go, to make a smooth batter.

2 Cut the potato skins into long slices, 5 mm (¼ in) thick, then cut the potatoes into rounds 5 mm (¼ in) thick. Drop the potato pieces – skins and rounds – into the batter and stir to coat them well.

3 Pour some oil into a *karhai*, wok or deep frying pan to a depth of 5 cm (2 in) and set it over a low to medium heat. When hot – it should reach 180°C (350°F) if you have a thermometer – take as many potato pieces as will fit in a single layer and scatter them evenly in the hot oil. Fry, stirring occasionally, for about 7 minutes or until they are golden on both sides. Remove the *bhajias* with a slotted spoon and spread them out on a large plate lined with kitchen paper to drain. Repeat with the remaining potato pieces and serve hot.

Chicken tikka with tomato

This is quite perfect with drinks for a large party. Just stick wooden cocktail sticks into the chicken pieces and pass the tray around.

serves 6–8
preparation time: 10 minutes,
 plus 4 hours' marinating
cooking time: 20 minutes

For the marinade:

5 tablespoons olive oil

3½ tablespoons red wine vinegar

1 onion, chopped

4 garlic cloves, chopped

2.5 cm (1 in) piece of fresh root ginger, chopped

2 tablespoons ground cumin

2 teaspoons ground coriander

seeds from 10 cardamom pods

1 teaspoon ground cinnamon

8 cloves

20 black peppercorns

1 teaspoon cayenne pepper

2 teaspoons salt

1 tablespoon tomato purée

1.5 kg (3 lb) skinned and boned chicken breasts

1 Put all the ingredients for the marinade in a food processor or blender and process to a smooth paste.

2 Cut the chicken breasts into strips 5 cm (2 in) long and 1 cm (½ in) wide. Put the chicken pieces in a bowl, add the marinade and stir to mix. Cover and chill for 4–5 hours.

3 Preheat the grill and line the grill pan with foil. Arrange about half the chicken on the foil in a single layer, leaving behind any marinade that does not cling to the meat. Grill the chicken for about 10 minutes or until there are

light-brown spots on the surface. Turn over the chicken pieces and grill for another 10 minutes, until lightly speckled. Transfer to a warm plate and cook the remaining chicken in the same way. Serve immediately.

Easy kebabs

When Indians and Pakistanis talk about their beloved kebabs, they are referring to a very large and varied family of dry (i.e., unsauced) meat dishes. Kebabs can be made like hamburgers out of minced raw meat (*chappali kebab*, for example) or patties could be made out of finely ground cooked meat and fried (such as the *shami kebab*). If minced meat is wrapped around a skewer before grilling it might be called a *seekh kebab*. If chicken chunks are marinated, skewered and cooked in a tandoor, the dish would be chicken *tikka*, which is yet another type of kebab. Often, thin slices of meat are marinated with spices and nuts and then cooked on a hot griddle or stone, as in this recipe. You may make these with lamb or beef, cut into thin slices.

serves 6–8
preparation time: 10 minutes,
 plus 2 hours' marinating
cooking time: 10–20 minutes

450 g (1 lb) tender beef or
 lamb steak

2 teaspoons very finely
 grated fresh root ginger

1 teaspoon finely crushed
 garlic

1–2 hot green chillies, very
 finely chopped

½ teaspoon ground cumin

½ teaspoon *garam masala*

¾ teaspoon salt

about 1 tablespoon olive oil

freshly ground black pepper

lime wedges and sprigs of
 mint, to serve

1 Cut the meat across the grain into very thin, neat slices, about 7.5 cm (3 in) long and 2.5 cm (1 in) wide. Put them into a bowl.

2 Add the ginger, garlic, chillies, cumin, *garam masala*, salt and lots of black pepper. Toss well to mix. Cover and set aside in the refrigerator for 2 hours or even overnight.

3 Brush a heavy frying pan, preferably cast iron, or a griddle with the oil and set it over a high heat. When it is very hot, lay as many meat slices in it as will fit easily in a single layer. Do not overcrowd the pan. When the meat has browned underneath, turn the slices over to brown the second side. Transfer to a warm serving plate and keep warm while you cook the remaining meat. Serve with lime wedges and sprigs of mint.

FISH and SHELLFISH

Grilled or *bhuna* fish steaks

This is a simple and lovely dish to make for guests or for the family. It is light, full of flavour and cooks quickly. I often serve it just with new potatoes and green beans. On days when I have a little more time I make Stir-fried cauliflower with green chillies (see page 90) and Potatoes with cumin (see page 94) instead.

serves 2–4

preparation time: 10 minutes, plus 15 minutes' marinating

cooking time: 10 minutes

For the marinade:

2 teaspoons very finely grated fresh root ginger

3 garlic cloves, crushed

1 teaspoon *garam masala*

½ teaspoon ground cumin

¼ teaspoon ground turmeric

½ teaspoon mustard powder

¼–½ teaspoon cayenne pepper

2 tablespoons lemon juice

¾ teaspoon salt, or to taste

freshly ground black pepper

5 tablespoons melted butter or olive oil, or a mixture of the two

675 g (1½ lb) thick fish steaks (or thick, skinless fish fillets), such as halibut, haddock, tuna, salmon or swordfish

1 Combine all the ingredients for the marinade in a bowl, adding a tablespoon or so of warm water to make a very thick paste.

2 Line the rack of the grill pan with foil. Brush it with 1 tablespoon of the oil or butter and place the fish steaks on top. Smother the fish on both sides with the marinade and set aside for about 15 minutes (no longer than 30 minutes). Meanwhile, preheat the grill.

3 Drizzle half the butter or oil over the fish and grill for about 5–6 minutes or until nicely browned. Turn the pieces over carefully, drizzle with the remaining butter or oil and brown the second side. Check the thickest part of the fish to see if it is cooked through. If not, turn off the grill but let the fish sit under it until it is done.

Madras fish curry

You could choose from a variety of fish for this dish: try thick, skinned fillets of mackerel, bluefish, haddock, sea bass or salmon, cut into 7.5 cm (3 in) chunks, or king fish or swordfish steaks – cut off the skin around them first, and ask your fishmonger to halve or quarter large steaks.

serves 4
preparation time: 20 minutes
cooking time: 20 minutes

1 onion, coarsely chopped

3–4 garlic cloves, coarsely chopped

2.5 cm (1 in) piece of fresh root ginger, chopped

2 tablespoons red wine vinegar

4 tablespoons olive or groundnut oil

¼ teaspoon cumin seeds

¼ teaspoon fennel seeds

12 fenugreek seeds

½ teaspoon ground coriander

½ teaspoon ground cumin

¼ teaspoon ground turmeric

2 canned tomatoes, finely chopped

½ teaspoon cayenne pepper, or more to taste

1 teaspoon *garam masala*

¾–1 teaspoon salt

200 ml (7 fl oz) water

675 g (1½ lb) fish (see above)

freshly ground black pepper

1 Put the onion, garlic, ginger and vinegar in a blender or food processor and blend to a smooth paste.

2 Put the oil into a large, wide pan, preferably non-stick, and set it over a medium-high heat. When it is very hot, put in the cumin, fennel and fenugreek seeds and let them sizzle for 5 seconds.

3 Quickly pour in the paste from the blender, using a rubber spatula to get it all out. Stir and fry it for 10–15 minutes, until it is golden brown.

4 Add the ground coriander, cumin and turmeric and stir for a minute.

5 Add the tomatoes, cayenne, *garam masala*, salt and lots of black pepper. Cook, stirring, for another 2–3 minutes.

6 Stir in the water and bring to the boil. Cover the pan, reduce the heat to low and simmer very gently for 30 minutes.

7 Add the fish in a single layer.
   Simmer gently, spooning the
   sauce over the fish, until it
   has just cooked through.

Fish in a green sauce

In India, all sorts of meat and fish are cooked in similar sauces. In the west Indian town of Surat, green sauce is used to cook liver. In my Delhi family, we often used to marinate lightly flattened pieces of boneless chicken breast in this sauce and then sauté them. Of course, it is absolutely ideal for fish, too. If you are using swordfish, remove the skin.

serves 2–4
preparation time: 15 minutes, plus 15 minutes' marinating
cooking time: 30 minutes

2 fish steaks (see above), about 675 g (1½ lb) in total, cut into halves or quarters

⅛ teaspoon ground turmeric

⅛ teaspoon cayenne pepper

3 tablespoons olive or groundnut oil

salt and freshly ground black pepper

For the green sauce:

½ teaspoon brown mustard seeds

1 tablespoon finely chopped shallots

2 teaspoons very finely grated fresh root ginger

3 garlic cloves, crushed to a pulp

1 large teacup finely chopped fresh coriander

1 tomato, finely chopped

2–3 green chillies, finely chopped

1 tablespoon lemon juice

about ¼ teaspoon salt

½ teaspoon *garam masala*

150 ml (¼ pint) water

1 Rub the fish all over with the turmeric, cayenne and some salt and pepper. Set aside for 15 minutes or longer (if longer, cover and refrigerate).

2 Put the oil in a large, wide frying pan, preferably non-stick, and set it over a high heat. When it is hot, put in the pieces of fish and brown them briefly on both sides (they will not cook through). Remove with a slotted fish slice and set aside.

3 Put the mustard seeds into the oil left in the pan. As soon as they begin to pop – a matter of seconds – add the shallots, ginger and garlic. Reduce the heat to medium-high and stir the seasonings until they are lightly browned. Stir in the coriander, tomato, green chillies, lemon juice, salt, *garam masala* and water. Turn the heat to low, cover and simmer for 10 minutes. Return the fish to the pan. Spoon some of the sauce over it and bring to a simmer. Cover and cook gently for 10 minutes or until the fish is cooked through.

Squid in a spicy spinach sauce

These days you can buy frozen cleaned squid from most supermarkets and Chinese grocers. If you buy fresh squid instead, see pages 19–20 for directions on cleaning it. After cleaning, cut the tubular body into rings 5 mm (¼ in) wide. The tentacles may be left whole or halved.

Serve this dish with plain rice or, as a refreshing change, over pasta! You could substitute prawns or cubes of salmon fillet for the squid if you prefer.

serves 4
preparation time: 20 minutes
cooking time: 35 minutes

3 tablespoons olive or groundnut oil

1 onion, chopped

3 garlic cloves, chopped

2.5 cm (1 in) cube of fresh root ginger, finely chopped

¼ teaspoon ground turmeric

1 teaspoon ground cumin

1 teaspoon ground coriander

1–1¼ teaspoons salt

3–4 hot green chillies, chopped

150 g (5 oz) canned chopped tomatoes

225 g (8 oz) fresh spinach, chopped

250 ml (8 fl oz) water

550 g (1¼ lb) prepared squid (see above)

freshly ground black pepper

1 Put the oil in a large, wide pan and set it over a medium-high heat. When it is hot, put in the onion, garlic and ginger. Cook, stirring, until the onion has browned lightly. Add the turmeric, cumin, coriander, salt and some black pepper and stir for 10 seconds.

2 Add the chillies, tomatoes and spinach and cook, stirring, for 3–4 minutes or until the spinach has wilted. Add the water and bring to the boil. Cover the pan, turn the heat to low and simmer gently for 20 minutes. Then blend the mixture coarsely, either with a hand-held blender in the pan or by whizzing it in a blender.

3 Just before serving, bring the puréed spinach mixture to the boil. Drop in the squid and simmer gently for 3–4 minutes, until it is just cooked through.

Prawns in a butter-tomato sauce

A very elegant dish, ideal for entertaining. Serve it with plain rice. The sauce can be made ahead of time and refrigerated, but the stir-frying is best done just before serving.

For the sauce:

1 tablespoon tomato purée

¾ teaspoon salt

¼ teaspoon sugar

1 teaspoon *garam masala*

½ teaspoon ground cumin

½ teaspoon cayenne pepper

1 tablespoon lemon juice

200 ml (7 fl oz) single cream

4 tablespoons water

2 tablespoons olive or groundnut oil

25 g (1 oz) unsalted butter

1 teaspoon cumin seeds

2 tablespoons finely chopped shallots

3 garlic cloves, finely chopped

550 g (1¼ lb) medium-sized raw prawns, peeled, de-veined (see page 19), then rinsed and patted dry

¼ teaspoon ground turmeric

1 teaspoon ground coriander

¼ teaspoon cayenne pepper

½ teaspoon salt

serves 4–5

preparation time: 20 minutes

cooking time: 10 minutes

1 Combine all the ingredients for the sauce in a bowl and whisk until smooth. Cover and chill until needed.

2 Put the oil and butter in a large frying pan and set over a high heat. When hot, add the cumin seeds and let them sizzle for 10 seconds. Put in the shallots and garlic and cook, stirring, until very lightly browned. Add the prawns, turmeric, coriander, cayenne and salt. Stir and fry until the prawns have just turned opaque.

3 Pour in the sauce and heat it through, stirring as you go. Serve immediately.

Stir-fried prawns with mustard seeds, garlic and mint

Prawns cook up so fast that I often use them for an easy meal. You need medium-sized, raw prawns here, the kind that are sold without their heads. I like to serve this dish with plain rice and a simple vegetable or a salad.

serves 3–4
preparation time: 15 minutes
cooking time: 5 minutes

4 tablespoons olive or groundnut oil

½ teaspoon brown mustard seeds

2 hot dried red chillies, each broken into 2–3 pieces

4 garlic cloves, finely chopped

450 g (1 lb) medium-sized raw prawns, peeled, de-veined (see page 19), then rinsed and patted dry

½ teaspoon salt

1 tablespoon finely chopped fresh mint

a few squeezes of lemon juice

1 Put the oil in a large frying pan and set it over a high heat. When it is very hot, put in the mustard seeds and red chillies. As soon as the mustard seeds start to pop – a matter of seconds – put in the garlic and stir for 3–4 seconds.

2 Add the prawns and salt. Stir and fry until the prawns turn completely opaque.

3 Stir in the mint and lemon juice to taste and serve immediately.

Goan prawn curry

One of India's favourite curries, this is also very simple to prepare. All you need are good-quality prawns. You could make an equally popular Goan fish curry using this recipe. Just replace the prawns with a large, thick fillet of haddock or salmon, cut into 4 cm (1½ inch) cubes.

Serve with plain rice.

serves 4
preparation time: 20 minutes
cooking time: 20 minutes

1 teaspoon cayenne pepper

1 tablespoon bright-red paprika

¼ teaspoon ground turmeric

2 tablespoons ground coriander

1 teaspoon ground cumin

1 tablespoon lemon juice

¾ teaspoon salt, or to taste

100 ml (3½ fl oz) water

3 tablespoons olive or groundnut oil

½ teaspoon brown mustard seeds

1 large shallot, cut into fine slivers

3 garlic cloves, cut into fine slivers

400 ml (14 fl oz) can of coconut milk, well stirred

450 g (1 lb) medium-sized raw prawns, peeled, de-veined (see page 19), then rinsed and patted dry

1 Put the cayenne, paprika, turmeric, coriander, cumin, lemon juice, salt and water in a bowl. Mix well to form a smooth paste and set aside. You can prepare this paste in advance of cooking the curry.

2 Put the oil into a large, deep frying pan and set it over a medium-high heat. When it is very hot, put in the mustard seeds. As soon as they begin to pop – a matter of seconds – add the shallot and garlic. Cook, stirring, until they are golden brown. Stir in the spice paste and bring to a simmer. Turn the heat to medium-low, then cover and simmer gently for 10 minutes.

3 Add the coconut milk and prawns and bring to a simmer over a medium-high heat. Once the sauce is bubbling, turn the heat low and simmer, uncovered, until the prawns have just turned opaque. Serve immediately.

Goan clams (or mussels)

In Goa this dish is served with rice. The rice absorbs the briny, garlicky, coconut-sweet, pungent-with-chilli juices, and the clams, mussels, or even cockles, go a long way. I like to serve them in a large soup plate with crusty bread on the side. The bread absorbs the juices, performing the same function as the rice.

serves 4
preparation time: 15 minutes
cooking time: 20 minutes

24 fresh clams or mussels

4 tablespoons olive oil

1 large onion, very finely chopped

7 garlic cloves, crushed to a pulp

2 teaspoons very finely grated fresh root ginger

2–3 hot green chillies, finely chopped (do not remove the seeds)

2 teaspoons ground cumin

½ teaspoon ground turmeric

½ teaspoon salt

400 g (14 oz) can of coconut milk, well stirred

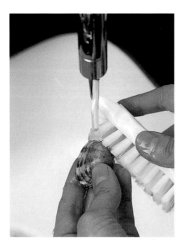

1 Scrub the clams or mussels well under cold running water with a plastic scrubbing brush, discarding any with open shells that do not close when tapped on the work surface. If you are using mussels, be sure to remove their trailing beards.

2 Put the oil in a large, wide pan and set it over a medium-high heat. When it is hot, put in the onion. Cook, stirring, until golden brown. Add the garlic, ginger and chillies and stir for another minute. Then add the cumin, turmeric and salt. Stir for 30 seconds.

3 Add the coconut milk and bring to the boil. Put in the clams or mussels, stir and return to the boil. Cover the pan tightly (with foil and the lid if necessary), and cook for 5–7 minutes over a medium heat, until the shells open. Discard any unopened shells and serve immediately.

EGGS, POULTRY and MEAT

'Indian-style' scrambled eggs

A favourite brunch dish, this is eaten in nearly all Indian homes in its myriad variations. You may serve it with crusty French bread, toast or any Indian bread. It is best to have all the ingredients prepared in advance. The actual cooking takes no time at all and should be done at the last minute.

serves 4
preparation time: 10 minutes
cooking time: 5 minutes

3 tablespoons unsalted butter or olive oil, or a mixture of the two

¼ teaspoon cumin seeds

2 mushrooms, coarsely chopped

2 spring onions, sliced into very fine rounds

1 hot green chilli, cut into fine rounds

3 tablespoons finely chopped tomato

1 tablespoon finely chopped fresh coriander

8 eggs, lightly beaten

salt and freshly ground black pepper

1 Put the butter and/or oil in a large frying pan, preferably non-stick, and set it over a medium-high heat. When it is hot, put in the cumin seeds and let them sizzle for 10 seconds. Add the mushrooms, spring onions and chilli and stir until the mushrooms are silky.

2 Put in the chopped tomato and coriander and stir for 30 seconds.

3 Add the eggs and some salt and pepper. Stir gently until the eggs form soft, thick curds and are done to your taste. Serve immediately.

Hard-boiled eggs in a rich Moghlai sauce

This is just perfect for a light supper and can be whipped up quite quickly. Here the sauce for the eggs is rich and creamy – hence the 'Moghlai' in the title (i.e., in the style of the Moghlai court). Serve with rice or any bread. I even love these eggs with toast.

serves 4
preparation time: 15 minutes
cooking time: 10 minutes

½ teaspoon cayenne pepper

1 teaspoon ground cumin

½ teaspoon *garam masala*

1 teaspoon ground coriander

1 tablespoon lemon juice

½–¾ teaspoon salt

2 tablespoons olive or groundnut oil

50 g (2 oz) onion, finely chopped

2.5 cm (1 in) piece of fresh root ginger, grated to a pulp

2 teaspoons tomato purée

150 ml (¼ pint) chicken stock

300 ml (½ pint) single cream

2 tablespoons chopped fresh coriander

6–8 hard-boiled eggs, peeled and cut lengthways in half

freshly ground black pepper

1 Mix the cayenne, cumin, *garam masala*, coriander, lemon juice, salt and some black pepper with 1 tablespoon of water in a cup. Set aside.

2 Put the oil in a large frying pan and set it over a medium-high heat. When it is hot, add the onion and stir-fry until it turns brown at the edges. Add the ginger and stir for 10 seconds, then add the paste from the cup and stir for 30 seconds. Stir in the tomato purée, chicken stock, cream and fresh coriander and bring to a simmer. Cover and simmer gently for 2–3 minutes.

3 Lay the egg halves in the
sauce in a single layer and
spoon the sauce over the
top. Cover and simmer
very gently for another
2–3 minutes, then serve.

Tandoori-style chicken

Since I do not have a tandoor at home, I use my oven turned up to the highest temperature it can manage to make this dish. Also, I have given up painting my tandoori chicken red. It tastes just as good without the artificial colouring and is much healthier besides.

serves 4
preparation time: 25 minutes, plus 8–24 hours' marinating
cooking time: 20–25 minutes

1.25 kg (2½ lb) chicken pieces (legs and/or breasts), skinned

1 teaspoon salt

3 tablespoons lemon juice

For the marinade:

450 ml (¾ pint) plain yoghurt

½ onion, coarsely chopped

1 garlic clove, chopped

2.5 cm (1 in) piece of fresh root ginger, chopped

1–2 hot green chillies, roughly sliced

2 teaspoons *garam masala*

lime or lemon wedges, to serve

1 Cut each chicken leg into 2 pieces and each breast into 4 pieces. Make 2 deep slits crossways on the meaty parts of each leg and breast piece. The slits should not start at an edge and should be deep enough to reach the bone. Spread the chicken pieces out on 2 large platters. Sprinkle one side with half the salt and half the lemon juice and rub them in. Turn the pieces over and repeat on the second side. Set aside for 20 minutes.

2 Meanwhile, make the marinade: combine the yoghurt, onion, garlic, ginger, chillies and *garam masala* in a blender or food processor and blend until smooth. Strain the paste through a coarse sieve into a large bowl, pushing through as much liquid as you can.

3 Put the chicken and all its accumulated juices into the bowl with the marinade. Rub the marinade into the slits in the meat, then cover and refrigerate for 8–24 hours. Preheat the oven to its maximum temperature and set a shelf in the top third of the oven where it is hottest. Remove the chicken pieces from the marinade and spread them out in a single layer on a large, shallow baking tray. Bake for 20–25 minutes, until cooked through. Lift the chicken pieces out of their juices and serve with lime or lemon wedges.

Chicken tikka masala

To make this recipe, you first have to make Tandoori-style chicken (see page 68) and then enfold it in a traditional curry sauce. In restaurants, it all tends to look rather red because of the food colouring. Here is my healthier version. When making the Tandoori-style chicken, remember to save the marinade and the cooking juices, as you will need them here.

serves 4
preparation time: 15 minutes, plus preparing the Tandoori-style chicken
cooking time: 20 minutes

5 tablespoons olive or groundnut oil

5 cardamom pods

5 cm (2 in) piece of cinnamon stick

2 onions, finely chopped

2 teaspoons finely grated fresh root ginger

2 teaspoons garlic, crushed to a pulp

1 teaspoon ground cumin

1 teaspoon ground coriander

¼ teaspoon ground turmeric

½–1 teaspoon cayenne pepper (depending how hot you like it)

1 tablespoon bright-red paprika

4 tablespoons of the reserved Tandoori-style chicken marinade

1 large tomato, very finely chopped

1 teaspoon tomato purée

1 teaspoon *garam masala*

150 ml (¼ pint) water

1 quantity of Tandoori-style chicken (see page 68)

¼ teaspoon salt

1 Put the oil into a large, wide pan and set it over a medium-high heat. When it is very hot, put in the cardamom pods and cinnamon stick. Stir once, then add the onions. Stir until they begin to turn brown at the edges. Add the ginger and garlic and cook, stirring, for 1 minute. Add the cumin, coriander, turmeric, cayenne and paprika and stir for 30 seconds.

2 Add the tandoori chicken marinade, a tablespoon at a time, and stir it in so it is absorbed by the spices.

3 Add the tomato, tomato purée and *garam masala* and cook, stirring, for a minute. Pour in the water and bring to a simmer. Cover, turn the heat to low and simmer gently for 10 minutes. Taste for salt, adding about ¼ teaspoon or as needed.

4 Add the cooked chicken and the juices from the baking tray. Raise the heat to high and fold the chicken into the sauce. The sauce should thicken and cling to the chicken pieces.

Creamy chicken korma with almonds

I happen to like dark chicken meat so, given a choice, I would use only chicken thighs for this recipe. However, many people prefer light meat, including two members of my own family. Whatever chicken pieces you choose, legs must be cut into two parts (drumstick and thigh) and breasts must be cut in half across the centre. If you prefer, you could use a whole chicken, cut into serving pieces and skinned.

serves 4
preparation time: 20 minutes
cooking time: 35 minutes

5–6 garlic cloves, coarsely chopped

2.5 cm (1 in) piece of fresh root ginger, chopped

50 g (2 oz) flaked almonds

5 tablespoons olive or groundnut oil

2 bay leaves

8 cardamom pods

4 cloves

2.5 cm (1 in) piece of cinnamon stick

1 onion, finely chopped

1 tablespoon ground cumin

1 tablespoon ground coriander

¼ teaspoon cayenne pepper

1 tablespoon tomato purée

1.5 kg (3 lb) chicken pieces, skinned and cut into serving portions (see above)

1¼ teaspoons salt

3 tablespoons single cream

½ tablespoon *garam masala*

150 ml (¼ pint) water

1 Put the garlic, ginger, almonds and 6 tablespoons of water into a blender and blend to a smooth paste. Put the oil in a wide pan and set it over a medium-high heat. When it is very hot, put in the bay leaves, cardamom pods, cloves and cinnamon stick and stir for 10 seconds. Add the onion and cook, stirring, until browned.

2 Reduce the heat to medium and add the paste from the blender, along with the cumin, coriander and cayenne. Stir for 3–4 minutes, then add the tomato purée and stir for a minute longer.

3 Add the chicken pieces, salt, cream, *garam masala* and water. Bring to a simmer, then cover the pan, turn the heat to low and simmer gently for 25 minutes, until the chicken is done.

Minced lamb with peas

Known in India as *Keema matar*, this dish has been a mainstay for young Indians abroad for decades now. While the mince can be made of cheaper cuts, good-quality meat yields a tastier *Keema*. You could use minced beef but I prefer lamb that is not too fatty. I like to combine the ground spices in a small cup before I start cooking, so that I do not have to put each one into the pan separately.

Serve with rice or Indian breads.

serves 4
preparation time: 10 minutes
cooking time: 50 minutes

4 tablespoons olive or groundnut oil

1 onion, finely chopped

2 teaspoons crushed garlic

1 tablespoon fresh root ginger, grated to a pulp

1 teaspoon ground cumin

1 teaspoon ground coriander

¼ teaspoon ground turmeric

¼ teaspoon ground cinnamon

¼ teaspoon ground nutmeg

½ teaspoon cayenne pepper

200 g (7 oz) tomatoes, chopped

4 tablespoons plain yoghurt

550 g (1¼ lb) minced lamb

1¼ teaspoons salt, or to taste

250 ml (8 fl oz) water

2 tablespoons lemon juice

150 g (5 oz) fresh or frozen peas

1 Put the oil in a large frying pan, preferably non-stick, and set it over a medium-high heat. When it is hot, add the onion, garlic and ginger and stir until lightly browned. Add the cumin, coriander, turmeric, cinnamon, nutmeg and cayenne pepper and stir for 10 seconds.

2 Stir in the tomatoes and yoghurt. Cook on a medium-high heat until the tomatoes have softened. Add the minced lamb and salt. Cook, stirring, for 2 minutes, breaking up all the lumps. Stir in the water and bring to a simmer, then cover, turn the heat to low and simmer for 30 minutes.

3 Add the lemon juice and peas to the pan. Return to a simmer, then cover once more and cook gently for 10 minutes.

Moghlai lamb korma with sultanas

This deliciously rich dish with its gentle sweet and sour flavour is perfect for entertaining, as it can be made in advance and stored in the refrigerator for 24 hours. Just reheat it before you sit down to eat.

Serve with rice or Indian breads.

serves 4–6
preparation time: 15 minutes
cooking time: 1¼ hours

250 ml (8 fl oz) plain yoghurt

1 teaspoon salt, or to taste

2 teaspoons ground cumin

1 teaspoon ground coriander

¼ teaspoon cayenne pepper, or to taste

4 tablespoons finely chopped fresh coriander

5 tablespoons olive or groundnut oil

5 cm (2 in) piece of cinnamon stick

1 bay leaf

6 cardamom pods

900 g (2 lb) boneless lamb from the shoulder, cut into 2.5–4 cm (1–1½ in) cubes

1 onion, finely chopped

4 tablespoons sultanas

2 tablespoons soured cream

¼ teaspoon ground cardamom

freshly ground black pepper

1 Put the yoghurt into a bowl and beat lightly until smooth. Add the salt, cumin, ground coriander, cayenne, lots of black pepper and the fresh coriander. Mix well and set aside.

2 Put the oil into a wide pan, preferably non-stick, and set it over a medium-high heat. When it is hot, add the cinnamon stick, bay leaf and cardamom pods. Quickly put in the lamb pieces – only as many as the pan will hold easily in a single layer – and brown them on all sides. Remove with a slotted spoon and put in a bowl. Brown all the meat in the same way.

3 Put the onion into the oil left in the pan. Cook, stirring, until it turns brown at the edges. Now return the meat to the pan, along with any whole spices that are still clinging to it, plus the yoghurt mixture and the sultanas. Stir well and bring to a simmer. Cover the pan, turn the heat to low and simmer gently for 1 hour or until the meat is very tender. Then uncover the pan and turn up the heat. Cook over a high heat, stirring, until the sauce is thick and clings to the meat pieces. Finally, stir in the soured cream, sprinkle the ground cardamom over the top and serve.

Lamb or beef jhal fraizi

Jhal fraizi was a speciality of the Anglo-Indians in India. Often the Calcutta mixed-race community would have a very English meal of roast lamb or roast beef on Sunday, then transform the leftovers into a spicy *jhal fraizi* on Monday, thus paying culinary homage to both sides of their ancestry.

serves 3–4
preparation time: 15 minutes
cooking time: 10 minutes

350 g (12 oz) cooked, boneless roast lamb or beef

3 tablespoons olive or groundnut oil

¼ teaspoon cumin seeds

¼ teaspoon brown mustard seeds

8 fenugreek seeds

100 g (4 oz) green pepper, cut lengthways into slivers 3 mm (⅛ in) thick

1–2 hot green chillies, cut into long, thin slivers (do not remove the seeds)

150 g (5 oz) onion, cut into thin half rings

1 teaspoon Worcestershire sauce

1 teaspoon ground cumin

1 teaspoon ground coriander

¼ teaspoon ground turmeric

¾ teaspoon salt

freshly ground black pepper

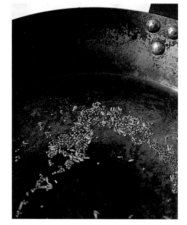

1 Cut the cooked meat into slivers, about 5 mm (¼ in) thick, 5 mm (¼ in) wide and 7.5 cm (3 in) long.

2 Put the oil in a large frying pan and set it over a medium-high heat. When it is very hot, put in the cumin, mustard and fenugreek seeds.

3 As soon as the mustard seeds begin to pop – a matter of seconds – put in the green pepper, chillies and onion. Fry, stirring, until the onion has browned and the mass of vegetables has reduced.

4 Add the meat, Worcestershire sauce, ground cumin, coriander, turmeric, salt and pepper. Cook, stirring, over a medium-high heat for 3–4 minutes, until the meat has heated through.

Taste for balance of seasonings, adding more of whatever you need.

Rogan josh

This gets its name from the paprika-like Kashmiri chillies that are used generously to give the dish a deep red colour (*rogan josh* implies that the dish is of a joyous, burnished red colour). I generally substitute good-quality, sweet, bright-red paprika and add a little cayenne to create the perfect heat. The fairly large amount of oil is necessary for making the sauce but any excess may be spooned off the top before serving.

You may make this dish with stewing beef if you like. You will need to extend the cooking time to about 1½ hours or until the beef is tender.

serves 4–6
preparation time: 15 minutes
cooking time: 1¼ hours

5 cm (2 in) piece of fresh root ginger, chopped

7 garlic cloves, chopped

6 tablespoons olive or groundnut oil

10 cardamom pods

2 bay leaves

2.5 cm (1 in) piece of cinnamon stick

900 g (2 lb) boneless lamb from the shoulder, cut into 2.5–4 cm (1–1½ in) cubes

200 g (7 oz) onions, finely chopped

2 teaspoons ground cumin

2 teaspoons ground coriander

1 teaspoon cayenne pepper

1½ tablespoons sweet, bright-red paprika

2 teaspoons tomato purée

1¼ teaspoons salt

300 ml (½ pint) water

1 Drop the ginger and garlic into a food processor or blender, add 4 tablespoons of water and blend to a paste. Put the oil into a wide pan, preferably non-stick, and set it over a medium-high heat. When it is hot, put in the cardamom pods, bay leaves and cinnamon stick. Quickly put in the lamb pieces – only as many as the pan will hold easily in a single layer – and brown on all sides. Remove with a slotted spoon and put in a bowl. Brown the remaining meat in the same way.

2 Add the onions to the oil left in the pan. Cook, stirring, until they turn brown at the edges. Add the paste from the blender and stir for 30 seconds. Next add to the pan the cumin, coriander, cayenne and paprika, stir once and then add the tomato purée. Stir for 10 seconds.

3 Add the meat and any whole spices that are still clinging to it, plus the salt and water. Stir well and bring to the boil. Cover the pan, turn the heat to low and simmer gently for 1 hour or until the meat is tender.

Lamb, pork or beef Madras

In the UK, Madras has come to mean a very hot curry and not much more. Here is a more authentic southern *porial*, which traditionally uses coriander seeds, peppercorns, fennel and fenugreek seeds in its spice mixture. It is quite hot as well, and quite delicious. It is always served with rice.

If you want to use pork, buy shoulder meat and cook it exactly like lamb. If you prefer beef, use good-quality stewing beef, add a little extra water and cook it for 1½ hours or until tender.

serves 4–6
preparation time: 20 minutes
cooking time: 1¼ hours

1 tablespoon coriander seeds

1 teaspoon black pepper-corns

1 teaspoon fennel seeds

10 fenugreek seeds

4 cloves

4 hot dried red chillies

6 tablespoons olive or groundnut oil

2 onions, very finely chopped

1 teaspoon very finely grated fresh root ginger

2 teaspoons crushed garlic

3–4 hot green chillies, very finely chopped

900 g (2 lb) boneless lamb from the shoulder, cut into 2.5–4 cm (1–1½ in) cubes

2 large tomatoes, very finely chopped

1½ teaspoons salt

400 ml (14 fl oz) can of coconut milk, well stirred

1 Put the coriander seeds, peppercorns, fennel seeds, fenugreek seeds, cloves and chillies into a small, cast-iron frying pan and set it over a medium heat. Stir the spices over the heat until they are a shade darker and give off a roasted aroma. Leave to cool, then grind in a clean spice grinder or coffee grinder.

2 Pour the oil into a wide pan, preferably non-stick, and set it over a medium-high heat. When it is hot, put in the onions and cook, stirring, until they turn brown at the edges. Add the ginger, garlic and green chillies and stir for 20 seconds. Add the meat and cook, stirring, for 5 minutes. Stir in the tomatoes, ground roasted spices, salt and coconut milk and bring to the boil.

3 Cover the pan, turn the heat to low and simmer gently for 1 hour or until the meat is tender. Uncover the pan and boil away a lot of the liquid, until a thick sauce clings to the meat.

VEGETABLES and ACCOMPANIMENTS

Tarka dal

Here I have combined two different *dals*, but you could use 175 g (6 oz) of just one of them. Serve with Plain basmati rice (see page 98) or an Indian bread.

serves 4
preparation time: 5 minutes
cooking time: 45 minutes

75 g (3 oz) yellow split peas (skinned *mung dal*)

75 g (3 oz) split red lentils (*masoor dal*)

½ teaspoon ground turmeric

900 ml (1½ pints) water

1–1¼ teaspoons salt

3 tablespoons olive or groundnut oil

½ teaspoon cumin seeds

2 hot dried red chillies

1 garlic clove, lightly crushed but left whole, then peeled

1 Put the two *dals* in a bowl and wash in several changes of water, then drain. Empty the *dals* into a heavy-based pan and add the turmeric and water. Stir and bring to the boil. Quickly (before the pan can boil over) turn the heat down low, then partly cover the pan and simmer gently for 40–45 minutes, until the *dals* are very soft. Stir in the salt, turn off the heat and cover the pan.

2 Put the oil in a small frying pan and set it over a medium-high heat. When it is very hot, put in the cumin seeds and chillies. As soon as the chillies darken – a matter of seconds – put in the garlic.

3 When the garlic has browned lightly, lift up the frying pan with one hand and, with the other, take the lid off the *dal* pan. Pour the contents of the frying pan – oil and spices – over the *dal* and then put the lid back on for a few minutes to trap the aromas.

Green lentils
with lemon slices

I often serve this when I entertain. While it is perfect with Indian meals, I have also served it with a roast leg of lamb!

serves 4
preparation time: 10 minutes
cooking time: 45 minutes

175 g (6 oz) green lentils

750 ml (1¼ pints) water

¾ teaspoon salt

3 tablespoons finely chopped fresh coriander

1 lemon

3 tablespoons olive or groundnut oil

½ teaspoon brown mustard seeds

2 hot dried red chillies

2 garlic cloves, lightly crushed but left whole, then peeled

1 Put the lentils and water in a heavy-based pan and bring to the boil. Partly cover the pan and cook for 40–45 minutes, until the lentils are very tender. Stir in the salt and fresh coriander, then turn off the heat. Now peel the lemon, removing all the white pith as well as the skin. Cut the lemon crossways into thin slices. Discard the small end slices and keep only the best eight of the large ones. Add them to the lentils and stir.

2 Heat the oil in a small frying pan over a medium-high heat. When it is very hot, put in the mustard seeds. As soon as they pop – a matter of seconds – put in the dried chillies. After a few seconds, when the chillies have darkened, add the garlic. Stir once or twice and then pour the contents of the frying pan over the lentils.

Stir-fried cauliflower with green chillies

Here rice grains are used as a spice. The secret of this dish lies in allowing the cauliflower pieces to brown. While it may be served with all Indian meals, I find that it goes equally well with a lamb or pork roast, with sausages and with grilled meats.

serves 3–4
preparation time: 10 minutes
cooking time: 10 minutes

3 tablespoons olive or
   groundnut oil

1 teaspoon any raw rice

½ teaspoon cumin seeds

450 g (1 lb) cauliflower florets

2.5 cm (1 in) piece of fresh
   root ginger, cut into fine
   rounds and then into
   fine slivers

2 hot green chillies, cut
   into long slivers (do not
   remove the seeds)

¾ teaspoon salt

½ teaspoon *garam masala*

¼ teaspoon ground turmeric

freshly ground black pepper

1 Put the oil into a *karhai* or wok and set it over a high heat. When it is hot, put in the rice and cumin seeds. Stir for a few seconds, until the rice is golden.

2 Quickly add the cauliflower florets, ginger and chillies. Stir and fry for 5–7 minutes, until the cauliflower has browned a little.

3 Add the salt, black pepper, *garam masala* and turmeric. Stir once and then add 4 tablespoons of water. Cover the *karhai*, reduce the heat to medium and cook for 2 minutes or until the cauliflower is just tender.

Mushroom and pea curry

A quick-cooking dish and one of my party favourites, this may be served with rice or Indian breads, along with a *dal* and a flavourful meat dish such as Rogan josh (see page 80).

Use frozen peas when fresh ones are not in season. Instead of water you could use chicken stock.

serves 4
preparation time: 10 minutes
cooking time: 10 minutes

4 tablespoons olive or groundnut oil

½ teaspoon cumin seeds

1 teaspoon finely chopped garlic

350 g (12 oz) medium-sized white mushrooms, cut lengthways into quarters

2 teaspoons very finely grated fresh ginger

2–3 hot green chillies, finely chopped

1 teaspoon ground coriander

1 teaspoon *garam masala*

1 tablespoon tomato purée

¾–1 teaspoon salt

150 g (5 oz) peas

2 tablespoons finely chopped fresh coriander

300 ml (½ pint) water

2 tablespoons soured cream

1 Put the oil in a large frying pan, preferably non-stick, and set it over a high heat. When it is hot, put in the cumin seeds and let them sizzle for 10 seconds. Add the garlic, stir once and then add the mushrooms, ginger and chillies. Cook, stirring, until the mushrooms turn silken.

2 Put in the ground coriander and *garam masala* and stir for 30 seconds. Then add the tomato purée, salt, peas, fresh coriander and water. Stir well and bring to the boil. Cover, turn the heat to low and simmer gently for 5 minutes.

3 Stir in the soured cream and cook gently for another minute, then serve.

Potatoes with cumin

Known in restaurants as *zeera aloo*, this is wonderful
with Indian breads, yoghurt *raitas* and pickles. It may also
be served with Western-style roasts.

450 g (1 lb) potatoes,
  unpeeled

3 tablespoons olive or
  groundnut oil

½ teaspoon cumin seeds

2 teaspoons very finely
  grated fresh root ginger

1 teaspoon salt

1 teaspoon ground cumin

½ teaspoon cayenne pepper

2 tablespoons finely chopped
  fresh coriander

freshly ground black pepper

serves 4
preparation time: 10 minutes
cooking time: 30 minutes

1 Cook the potatoes in boiling
salted water until tender, then
drain and leave to cool. Peel
and cut them into 2 cm (¾ in)
dice.

2 Put the oil in a large frying
pan, preferably non-stick,
and set it over a medium-
high heat. When it is very hot,
put in the cumin seeds and
fry for 10 seconds. Put in the
potatoes, ginger, salt, ground
cumin, cayenne and black
pepper.

3 Stir and fry the potatoes for
10 minutes, mashing them
lightly with a spatula. Stir in
the coriander and serve.

Moghlai spinach with browned shallots

Moghlai recipes for vegetables are often quite simple but utterly delicious. Here just a small amount of browned shallot slivers provides much of the flavour.

To cut a shallot into slivers, first cut it lengthways into halves or quarters, going parallel to its flattest side (a lot will depend upon size, of course). Now cut lengthways again, into fine, long slivers.

> serves 4
> preparation time: 15 minutes
> cooking time: 10 minutes

500 g (1 lb 2 oz) spinach

3 tablespoons olive or groundnut oil

2 hot dried red chillies

25 g (1 oz) shallot, cut into fine slivers

½ teaspoon salt

½ teaspoon sugar

½ teaspoon *garam masala*

4 tablespoons single cream

1 Wash the spinach and remove any large stalks. Cut the spinach leaves into wide ribbons if they are large, or leave them whole if small.

2 Put the oil in a *karhai*, wok or large frying pan and set it over a high heat. When it is hot, put in the chillies and stir quickly once or twice until they darken. Immediately add the slivers of shallot. Stir and fry over a medium-high heat until they brown.

3 Add the spinach, salt, sugar and *garam masala*. Stir well and cook until the spinach has wilted completely.

4 Add the cream and cook,
stirring, for 4–5 minutes,
then serve.

Plain basmati rice

There are many methods of cooking basmati rice so that every grain is separate and fully extended. I prefer the absorption method, which uses a minimum amount of water. The rice ends up cooking in steam.

A heavy pan with a tight-fitting lid is essential here. If you do not have a well-fitting lid, stretch a piece of foil across the top of the pan and crimp the edges around it, then put the lid on top of the foil.

serves 4
preparation time: 5 minutes,
 plus 30 minutes' soaking
cooking time: 25 minutes

basmati rice, measured to
 the 450 ml (¾ pint) level in
 a measuring jug
600 ml (1 pint) water

1 Wash the rice in several changes of water, then drain. Put it in a bowl, cover with water and leave to soak for 30 minutes, then drain again.

2 Empty the rice into a medium-sized, heavy pan (with a tight-fitting lid). Add the 600 ml (1 pint) water and bring to the boil. Cover tightly, turn the heat to very low and cook for 25 minutes.

Vegetable pullao

A vegetable *pullao* looks perfectly elegant when served at a formal dinner with meats and *dals* but it also looks quite at ease served with scrambled eggs for brunch, or plain yoghurt for breakfast. The vegetables in this *pullao* may be varied according to the season.

serves 4–6
preparation time: 15 minutes, plus 30 minutes' soaking
cooking time: 30 minutes

basmati rice, measured to the 450 ml (¾ pint) level in a measuring jug

3 tablespoons olive or groundnut oil

½ teaspoon brown mustard seeds

1 hot green chilli, finely chopped

100 g (4 oz) potato, peeled and cut into 5 mm (¼ in) dice

½ carrot, peeled and cut into 5mm (¼ in) dice

40 g (1½ oz) green beans, cut into 5 mm (¼ in) segments

½ teaspoon ground turmeric

1 teaspoon *garam masala*

1 teaspoon very finely grated fresh root ginger

1¼ teaspoons salt

600 ml (1 pint) water

1 Wash the rice in several changes of water, then drain. Put it in a bowl, cover with water and leave to soak for 30 minutes, then drain again. Put the oil in a heavy-based pan (with a tight-fitting lid) and set it over a medium-high heat. When it is hot, put in the mustard seeds. As soon as they begin to pop – a matter of seconds – put in the chilli, potato, carrot, green beans, turmeric, *garam masala* and ginger. Sauté, stirring, for 1 minute.

2 Reduce the heat to medium-low and add the drained rice and the salt. Cook the rice gently, stirring, for 2 minutes.

3 Add the water and bring to the boil. Cover the pan tightly with a close-fitting lid or with foil and a lid, then turn the heat to very low and cook for 25 minutes.

Yoghurt raita with cucumber and mint

Raitas are yoghurt relishes that can be made with fruit such as bananas and mangoes, with vegetables such as courgettes and cucumbers, with herbs such as mint and coriander, with dumplings, nuts, and with all manner of spices. They add both nutritional value and flavour to all Indian meals.

serves 4–6
preparation time: 5 minutes

450 ml (¾ pint) plain yoghurt

½–¾ teaspoon salt

¼ teaspoon cayenne pepper

10 cm (4 in) piece of
    cucumber, peeled
    and grated

2 tablespoons finely chopped
    fresh mint

1 Put the yoghurt in a bowl and beat lightly until smooth and creamy. Add the salt and cayenne and mix well.

2 Fold in the grated cucumber and chopped mint.

Fresh green chutney

A very refreshing chutney, full of vitamins. I serve it with most Indian meals. You should also try it in a cheese sandwich (smear it on the bread instead of butter!).

serves 6
preparation time: 10 minutes

6 tablespoons plain yoghurt

1 tablespoon lemon juice

2 heaped tablespoons finely chopped fresh mint

2 heaped tablespoons finely chopped fresh coriander

1 tablespoon finely chopped hot green chilli

⅓ teaspoon salt, or to taste

1 Put 4 tablespoons of the yoghurt in a bowl and beat lightly until smooth and creamy.

2 Put the lemon juice, remaining yoghurt, mint, coriander, chilli and salt into a blender and blend until smooth. Empty this mixture into the bowl with the yoghurt and mix well.

Tomato and onion cachumbar

Almost every Indian meal is served with a mini salad. At its simplest, this can take the form of a sliced raw onion or wedges of cucumber.

serves 4
preparation time: 10 minutes

100 g (4 oz) onion, cut into 1 cm (½ in) dice

350 g (12 oz) tomatoes, cut into 1 cm (½ in) dice

3 tablespoons finely chopped fresh coriander

3 tablespoons lemon juice

1½ teaspoons salt, or to taste

¼–½ teaspoon cayenne pepper (depending how hot you like it)

1 Put all the ingredients in a bowl and mix well.

Flaky flatbreads with cumin seeds

These flatbreads are known as *parathas*. As you make them, stack them on a large plate and cover them with a matching but upturned plate. They will stay warm for a good 30 minutes this way. If you wish to reheat them, put the whole stack of *parathas* (minus the plates) on a large sheet of foil and then fold over the foil to cover them well and form a tight packet. Put the packet in a moderate oven for 15–20 minutes. You can heat individual *parathas* for 1 minute or less in a microwave.

> makes 8
> preparation time: 40 minutes, plus 30 minutes for the dough to rest
> cooking time: 15–20 minutes

300 g (11 oz) *chapati* flour (or a half and half mixture of sifted wholemeal flour and plain white flour)

¾ teaspoon salt

1 teaspoon cumin seeds, lightly crushed in a mortar

2 teaspoons very finely chopped green chillies

2 tablespoons very finely chopped fresh coriander

2 tablespoons olive or groundnut oil

250 ml (8 fl oz) water

1 teaspoon very finely grated fresh root ginger

50–75 g (2–3 oz) melted butter or *ghee*

freshly ground black pepper

1 Combine the flour, salt, black pepper, cumin seeds, chillies and coriander in a large bowl and drizzle the oil over the top. Rub the oil and seasonings into the flour with your fingers.

2 Put the water in a cup and stir in the ginger. Slowly add enough water to the flour mixture to make a soft but manageable dough, mixing and kneading as you do so – you will need anything from 175 ml (6 fl oz) to all of the gingery water. Knead the dough – either in the bowl or on a work surface – for about 10 minutes, until smooth.

3 Put the dough in a bowl and cover with clingfilm or a damp tea-towel. Set aside for 30 minutes, then knead the dough again and divide it into 8 balls. Flatten each ball slightly to make a patty.

4 Set an Indian *tava*, cast-iron griddle or cast-iron frying pan on a medium-high heat. Give it time to get very hot. Meanwhile, dust your work surface and rolling pin with flour. Roll out one dough patty into a 15 cm (6 in) round. Drizzle 1 teaspoon of the melted butter or *ghee* over the surface and spread it evenly with the back of the teaspoon.

5 Fold one end of the round over itself in such a way that a third of the round is still uncovered. Then fold the uncovered end over the rest to form a rectangle of sorts. Drizzle ½ teaspoon of melted butter or *ghee* over the rectangle and spread it out with the back of the spoon.

6 Fold this rectangle over itself in such a way that a third is left exposed. Now fold the third over the rest to make a small square. Roll out this square into a much larger one, about 14–15 cm (5½–6 in) on each side. You may need to dust it with flour now and then.

7 Lift up the *paratha* and slap it into the centre of the hot pan. Cook for 30 seconds or until the dough turns white on top and light brown spots appear on the bottom.

8 Spread 1 teaspoon of melted butter or *ghee* over the top of the *paratha* and turn it over. Cook it for another 15 seconds. Turn the *paratha* 4 more times, every 15 seconds, without adding any more melted butter or ghee. The *paratha* is done when it has light brown spots, is slightly crisp on the outside and soft (but cooked through) on the inside. Make the remaining *parathas* in the same way.

Deep-fried puffed breads

The ideal flour to use for these breads, commonly known as *pooris*, is the fine wheatmeal flour sold by Indian grocers as *chapati* flour. It is best if the *pooris* are eaten as soon as they are made, or within 10 minutes. If you cannot do that, stack them as they are cooked in a foil-lined tin or plastic container and keep them covered. They will deflate and lose their crispness but will still taste very good.

makes 12
preparation time: 40 minutes, plus 10 minutes for the dough to rest
cooking time: 12 minutes

225 g (8 oz) *chapati* flour (or a half and half mixture of sifted wholemeal flour and plain white flour)

½ teaspoon salt

2 tablespoons groundnut oil, plus more for deep-frying

100–120 ml (3½–4 fl oz) water

1 Put the flour and salt in a bowl. Drizzle the 2 tablespoons of oil over the top and rub it in with your fingers.

2 Slowly mix in enough of the water to form a medium-soft ball of dough. Turn out and knead for about 10 minutes, until smooth.

3 Shape the dough into a ball, rub it with a little oil, and set aside in a covered bowl. Leave to rest for 10 minutes or longer.

4 Put some oil into a *karhai* or small wok to a depth of at least 5 cm (2 in) and set it over a medium-high heat. Allow it to get very hot. Meanwhile, divide the dough into 12 balls. Take one ball (keep the rest covered) and roll it out into a 13 cm (5 in) disc, flouring the work surface to prevent sticking if necessary.

5 Immediately, lift up the disc and carefully lay it on top of the hot oil without letting it fold up on itself. It will begin to float and sizzle, and will puff up in seconds.

6 Using a slotted spoon, flick oil over the *poori*, using light, gentle and quick strokes. Turn the *poori* over and cook it for another few seconds.

7 Remove it with a slotted spoon and keep on a plate lined with kitchen paper. Make the remaining *pooris* in the same way.

Mango lassi

This cool, smooth drink is a delicious thirst-quencher. You could use fat-free yoghurt, if you prefer. Out of season, use good-quality, canned Alphonso mango slices or purée instead of fresh mango.

serves 2
preparation time: 5 minutes

250 ml (8 fl oz) plain yoghurt

150 g (5 oz) chopped, non-fibrous flesh from a peeled, ripe mango

2 tablespoons caster sugar

10 ice cubes

a few drops of rose water (optional)

2 sprigs of fresh mint

3 Pour the *lassi* into 2 glasses. Decorate with the sprigs of mint and serve.

1 Combine all the ingredients except the mint in a blender and blend until smooth.

2 Strain through a sieve, pushing through as much liquid as possible.

Menus

The secret of cooking an Indian meal successfully lies in preparing what you can easily, without too much strain. If you have never cooked Indian food before, find one simple recipe that you like and make it all by itself. You could start with the 'Indian-style' scrambled eggs on page 64, for example. Have them with toast. Buy only the spices that you need for that one dish. Do not let yourself get overwhelmed.

Once you have mastered your first recipe and gained some confidence, move on to another one and then another. Serve some Indian potatoes with your roast chicken. Or put some green chutney in a cheese sandwich. As your repertoire grows, so will the number of Indian spices in your kitchen cupboard.

If you decide to cook a more complicated meat dish, make some plain rice and a yoghurt *raita* to go with it. The meat and the *raita* can be prepared ahead of time. Your worries will be out of the way.

Unless snacks are being served with drinks, or soup is being served as a first course, most Indian dishes come to the table all at the same time. Traditionally, there is a meat, a vegetable, rice or bread, a *dal* and a relish (which could be a store-bought chutney or plain yoghurt). Sometimes there is no meat at all. 'Desserts', at mealtimes, generally consist of fresh seasonal fruit.

Family Dinner for 4

This is my idea of a perfect family meal. You could add some plain yoghurt, as well as some sliced tomato and cucumber. All the dishes can be made in advance and reheated just before eating.

Rogan josh

Potatoes with cumin

Flaky flatbreads with cumin seeds

Elegant Dinner Party for 6

This makes a really elegant meal and is quite manageable. The lamb, lentils, spinach and *cachumbar* can all be made in advance (double the spinach recipe to serve 6). Soak the rice 2 hours before your guests are due to arrive and begin cooking it 30 minutes after soaking. Leave the covered pan of cooked rice in a warm place or in a warming oven.

Moghlai lamb korma with sultanas

Green lentils with lemon slices

Plain basmati rice

Moghlai spinach with browned shallots

Tomato and onion cachumbar

Easy Dinner Party for 6

The mulligatawny soup can be made ahead and refrigerated, as can the base of the prawn curry. To serve 6, increase the amount of prawns to 675 g (1½ lb) but leave the sauce the way it is. Fold the prawns into the sauce at the last minute. Make the cauliflower earlier in the day and reheat it before serving. I like to start cooking my rice no more than an hour before guests arrive, so it stays hot. Store-bought chutneys and pickles may be added to the menu.

Easy mulligatawny soup

Goan prawn curry

Stir-fried cauliflower with green chillies

Plain basmati rice

Dinner Buffet for 20

I have chosen chicken here as most people will eat it. You will need to make five times the recipe. It is better to have too much than too little. Do five times the *dal*, three times the rice and four times the chutney. Store-bought pickles may be added to the menu. The chicken and *dal* can be made in advance.

Creamy chicken korma with almonds

Tarka dal

Plain basmati rice

Fresh green chutney

Vegetarian Dinner for 6

This is a very comforting meal. Make the *dal*, mushroom curry and *raita* ahead of time. The poppadums may also be fried in advance, left to cool on kitchen paper and then put in a large biscuit tin lined with fresh kitchen paper. Soak the rice 2 hours before guests are due to arrive, following the instructions for the Elegant Dinner Party for 6.

Fried poppadums

Tarka dal

Mushroom and pea curry

Vegetable pullao

Yoghurt raita with cucumber and mint

Sunday Lunch for 4

This simple meal can easily be expanded to feed more guests. Buy some ready made *nans* or pitta breads to accompany the chicken. Double the *lassi* recipe. If you like, you could have beer or lager instead of the *lassi*, or offer both.

Mango lassi

Tandoori-style chicken

Tomato and onion cachumbar

Dinner for 4 Seafood Lovers

Our family loves fish and on our annual holiday by the sea we fish off the coast and rake up clams. These are the dishes we cook for ourselves and our guests.

Goan clams (or mussels)

Fish in a green sauce

Plain basmati rice

Index

Where to buy good Indian food

Many Indian ingredients are now readily available in supermarkets, but to find the best suppliers, it is always worth asking Indian friends where they shop for groceries, or even consult your local curry restaurant! In most UK cities, you will find a wealth of convenience stores and Asian grocers offering a wide range of ingredients. Mail order and the Internet are excellent options and the number of food-related web sites is booming. Here are a few stockists and suppliers to point you in the right direction:

Ambala Sweet Centre
112–14 Drummond Street, London NW1
Tel: 020 7387 3521
This central London branch of Ambala stocks traditional Indian confectionary and other regional specialities. Drummond Street is home to numerous stores where you can pick up Indian ingredients.

Asian Food Centre
175–7 Staines Road, Hounslow, Middlesex TW3 3LF
Tel: 020 8570 7346
Fax: 020 8577 9301

Bhullar Brothers Ltd
44 Springwood Street, Huddersfield HD1 4BE
Tel: 01484 531607

Bristol Sweet Mart
80 St Mark's Road, Bristol BS5 6JH
Tel: 0117 951 2257 (retail)   0117 951 0690 (wholesale)
Fax: 0117 952 5456
http://sweetmart.co.uk
The Majothi family business began in 1978 and today encompasses three shops and an extensive online ordering service. They stock 5500 ingredients, and will obtain specialist foods from all over the world, including organic rice and sauces.

Chilli Willie's Spices by Post
http://www.curryhouse.co.uk/cw/index.htm
This web site offers online ordering of a variety of spices and other foods.

The Curry Club
http://www.curryclub.co.uk
Features useful links to general Indian food sites.

Deepak Cash & Carry
953–9 Garratt Lane, London SW17 0ND
Tel: 020 8767 7819
193 Upper Tooting Road SW17 7TG
Tel: 020 8672 7531
Basic but useful supermarkets stocking dried goods, including rice and pulses, breads, frozen vegetables, meat and fish, and cooking equipment.

The Food Hall
22–4 Turnpike Lane, London N8 0PS
Tel: 020 8889 2264
Fax: 020 8889 4432.

International Foods Store
83-95 Derby Road
Southampton
SO14 0DQ
Tel: 023 8039 9750
Stockists of Indian spices, sauces and utensils.

Mr Bell's
Old English Market, Cork
This stall in the Old English Market in Cork supplies spices and ethnic ingredients to the famed Ballymaloe Cookery School.

Oriental Food Stores
303 Great Western Road, Glasgow G4 9HS
Tel: 0141 400 2133

Quality Foods
47–61 South Road, Southall, Middlesex UB1 1SQ
Tel: 020 8917 9188
Grocer's stocking a huge range of Indian fruit and vegetables, alongside flours, spices and pickles. Southall is an important Asian shopping centre – there are myriad shops where you will find every Indian ingredient you could conceivably ever need!

Other titles in this series

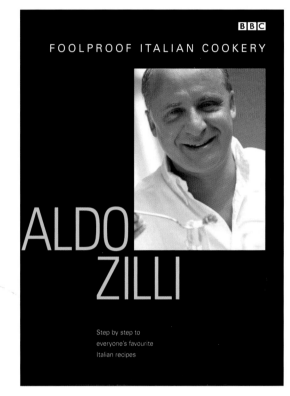

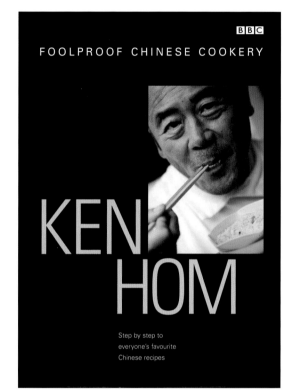

Bring the tastes and colours of Italy to your home with Aldo Zilli's delicious and easy-to-follow recipes. The top chef and restaurateur guides you through a stunning collection of Italian starters, soups, risottos, pasta sauces, meat and fish dishes and desserts, with mouthwatering recipes including *Seared tuna Sicilian style*, *Baby chicken diavola* and the classic *Tiramisu*.

Chinese food is popular the world over. In *Foolproof Chinese Cookery*, Ken Hom proves that anyone can cook this healthy and delicious cuisine. Here, he demonstrates 40 popular and well-known dishes, from *Spicy Sichuan-style prawns* to the more elaborate *Peking duck*. With his simple instructions, even the novice cook can make perfect steamed rice every time!